# The 4 KaMIT Codes

# DORRIS
# BOGUS

# The 4 KaMIT Codes

The path to balance, well-being, and joy.

To Houston, Alisha, Alyson, and Houston III:

You continue to contribute to my well-being. You bring balance

and joy to my world.

# CONTENTS

# ACKNOWLEDGEMENT

Thank you, mom, for bringing a Remington typewriter into our home. I used it to express my inner-most thoughts and feelings during my jr. high school years. I love you.

To my husband and three children, thank you for your support in all my adventures. I love you all. To my entire family, thank you for your part in shaping my resilient foundation. I love you.

Dedication:

To everyone who aspires to live a life of balance, well-being, and joy. Here's to an amazing life.

# Joy is Purple

Joy is purple in every glorious shade,

With the love of joy

That's how all things are made.

A heart full of joy smiles at life,

Gives a playful nod and a wink to stress and strife.

When challenges or problems come your way,

Skip, dance about and chase them away.

Because joy is purple in every glorious shade.


Author: Dorris Bogus

What color is your joy?

The 4 KaMIT Codes

# INTRODUCTION

This book is the result of listening to people from all levels of society who are trying to balance various roles while maintaining a sense of self. Common roles like spouse, parent, student, professional, employee and caregiver were consuming their lives. More than half of the people that I spoke with expressed the fear that if they put too much emphasis on one role, other equally important ones would suffer.

This often led to a constant state of frustration and guilt. Their solution was to multi-task; to juggle separate roles at once, which seemed to work for a while. Later they realized that they checked off daily activities from their to-do list, but without any conscience connection or meaning. There was no joy in what they were accomplishing. They had lost contact with what made them happy, fulfilled, self- accepted and at peace. Many had forgotten who they were at their human core.

When asked what a realistic, workable solution to leading a balanced lifestyle looked like, most said, "if I could just get that intangible thing, life would balance itself out, and only then would I have time to really live my dreams." That intangible thing was unique for each person. They were waiting for the right time and the perfect situation to start living their ideal life, while life continued all around them.

One of the challenges that I uncovered while speaking with people was that they did not know of any practical ways to start living their ideal life. They equated an ideal lifestyle with hard to obtain dreams, lucky breaks, or wealth. The 4 KaMIT Codes offer another perspective on how to live your life in balance, well-being, and joy. They focus on life-scaping principles and practical solutions to living in balance.

Life-scaping; (shaping and cultivating the vital elements in the environment of your life) can be overwhelming but certainly do-able. The 4 KaMIT Codes have the solution: which is to refocus and prioritize.

The 4 KaMIT Codes address the difficulty in balancing priorities. There are four principles that give you a framework to build and live your life in balance, well-being, and joy. That is what living life fully and out large is all about.

The 4 KaMIT Codes lead you on a journey of self-discovery where you identify the foundational elements that are vital to your ideal lifestyle framework. As your life expands and con-tracts, the framework that you build using the 4-KaMIT Codes will allow for the inevitable stress of change. They will help you maintain your balance, keep you joyful, and uncover what you need on a mental, physical, and spiritual level to live in well-being balance, and joy.

Live A Life of Wellbeing, Balance, and Joy!

Live A Life of Wellbeing, Balance, and Joy!

CODE 1

Self/

"The personality or character that makes a person different from other people: the combination of emotions, thoughts, feelings, and actions that make a person unique, among others."

# KaMIT CODE 1:

# TAKE CARE OF YOURSELF

You express the embodiment of KaMIT Code 1 in the way that you take care of yourself.

Consider taking care of yourself as a gift and a privilege. "It's not something you need to earn, it's a birthright."

Live A Life of Wellbeing, Balance, and Joy!

# CODE 1

# Take Care of Yourself

The first KaMIT Code, Take Care of Yourself, is the GOLDEN CODE. This code helps establish and ground you in self-awareness. It acts as an anchor that stabilizes your sense of self throughout your life. If you do not embrace this code, you will not function at your highest potential. When you put yourself first, you come from a place of fullness. From that state, you naturally give your best.

Taking care of yourself is vital, so you must make it a priority. Life demands attention; people, situations, and events will challenge you for your physical and mental time and energy. Practicing self-care does not come naturally or easily to most people. It becomes harder to learn to do so the more roles and obligations that we must fulfill. There are as many reasons as there are individual unique situations, but three common ones are:

**I: Impossible self-imposed standards:** What I call the 3-S Syndrome. Super- Self- Sufficiency Syndrome: I can do everything without any help from anyone. I can be all things to all. I've got it all under control.

**II: Society's ideals:** This is what I must look like and act like, for me to be "normal."

**III: Real, day-to-day obligations** to family, jobs, home, health, etc.

The ability to come to a point in your life where you decide to make you a priority depends on two main factors: how well you believe in, accept, and prioritize your highest aspirations and how well you resist critical self-talk. That can be difficult because often, you get your self-esteem from the roles you identify as your own and how others perceive you.

The roles you play validate your feelings of self-worth. You no doubt receive positive affirmations and genuine expressions of gratitude from fulfilling your roles. Positive affirmations are powerful motivators to continue in those roles even when they are no longer fulfilling or allow you to grow.

Once you find the courage to put your needs ahead of others, criticism might replace those positive affirmations that you previously received. Due to unconscious conditioning, negative thoughts in the form of self-blame take over and you may revert to the old habit of putting your needs behind others. Why does that happen?

Common reasons are fear of change, and self- doubt. You may not trust or value your own wants and needs. You may believe that putting yourself first means that you are selfish, cold-hearted, uncaring, or unaware of others' needs. Ask yourself, where did these beliefs come from? Are they my own or did they come from outside sources? The way to stop reacting to outside criticism with self- blame and doubt is to decide what is more important, your self-care or their beliefs about you. Are you giving them too much power over how you live your life? If the answer is yes, it is time to practice giving love, praise, and empathy to yourself. Start tuning into your own needs and wants. Turning inward means being consciously aware of your emotions as you make decisions about your life, and what the impact will be to your well-being. You must determine your own ideal of what makes you happy and why. It all comes down to what you value more, your own well-being, or momentary conditional praise from others. After strongly identifying with the roles of spouse, child, parent, etc., you may not know what your "you" role looks, feels, and acts like. The question is how do you begin to discover you? When you connect with your emotions you gain clarity and confidence in your decisions on how to move forward.

KaMIT-Code 1 is about self-discovery and writing your own life script. Self-care is an important part of that framework. It is a major building block in the construction of a balanced life. It begins with you assessing some foundational aspects of well-being and joy. These foundational aspects of well-being directly impact the quality of the framework of your life. The foundational elements allow you to build a framework based on your life's aspirations. These foundational elements should be unique to your needs and supportive of a balanced, dynamic, joyful, workable life.

Self- discovery /self -assessment begins by contemplating your current lifestyle and journaling your insights. Journaling is a tool that is beneficial; it allows you to be a third party looking in on your life without judging and you can critically review your life from an almost clinical perspective. It is like confiding in yourself.

Journaling your thoughts and daily activities helps you clarify where you are and how to set goals that are in your best interest.

# The Four KaMIT Codes

.

In your KaMIT Codes Companion Journal, record for one month how much time you engage in each of the foundational elements listed below. Add any foundational elements that are personal for you. These activities are foundational and therefore not optional. They are necessary building blocks for constructing a solid framework for self-care and well-being.

A: DOWN TIME.

B: EXERCISE.

C: NUTRITION

D: RECREATION WITH FAMILY AND FRIENDS.

E: WORK.

F: SPIRITUAL PRACTICE.

Live A Life of Wellbeing, Balance, and Joy!

This gives you a snapshot of how much time you focus on taking care of your basic foundational needs. Multiply the data from each foundational aspect by twelve to get a full year of insight. Ask yourself, "am I allowing myself enough time to build a healthy mental and physical foundation?" Again, this is a snapshot, so allow for seasonal changes in schedules. Here is where you get to write your own personalized script because no two life circumstances are alike.

How much "you time" is a reasonable ideal for your lifestyle or the lifestyle that you want to have? Select a basic foundational aspect of KaMIT-Code 1 that you want to improve. From your baseline assessment, set a measurable goal and create a *plan* that you can work into your ideal lifestyle. In formulating a plan, important questions to ask yourself are, why is it important to me?

How does it contribute to my well-being? What happens if I reach my goal? What will my life look like? What happens if I do not? "What am I willing to do to reach my goal but more importantly what are my limits?" "What am I willing to release or sacrifice to reach my goal?" Be clear and realistic about this part of your plan. In the long term, it is better to build on small incremental goals than to collapse under the weight of large unrealistic ones. As you gain insight into what works for your lifestyle you can set larger goals.

NUTRITION For example, if you want to focus on nutrition by eating healthier foods, *plan* for and set goals to have them available. Educate yourself about what you eat. Read food labels and research alternative, healthier ways to prepare your meals. Buy fresh seasonal food when available. Prepare a shopping list instead of shopping without one. Look at the list and circle the unhealthy choices. Set a goal to eliminate one food that is unhealthy from that list. For every unhealthy food that you eliminate replace it with a healthier option. Gradually increase that amount until you have reached your healthy pantry goal. Write all of this down in your KaMIT Codes Companion Journal.

EXERCISE: If your exercise goal is three times per week, where and when must be pre-arranged. Where in your schedule will you carve out the time and place? Start where you are. Whether you like to walk or do something more challenging, the key is to *plan,* set goals and start.

The goal is to start moving in any way that is physically possible. This will require deleting other activities from your schedule. Are you ready for the consequences, good or bad? Journaling your workouts and eating habits are important for two main reasons: 1) you are more likely to work out and eat healthier foods when you write them down and 2) you can look back and see the progress you have made and assess where you need to make improvements. Always consult your physician before starting an exercise plan or making any drastic changes to your diet.

> "I know that there are fitness trackers out there and they are wonderful, but if you want to connect the heart, mind and body then pick up a pen and write it down."

DOWN TIME As a busy mom, wife, and business owner, my favorite two questions were and still are, "is anybody bleeding or dying" and "will the sun stop shining if I do not do something right this minute?"

Those questions allowed me to be guilt free about leaving the office early, not attending all school functions, and not accompanying my spouse on a trip. Saying no, when necessary, will remove items from your plate and allow more down time for you. Have a plan for when and where you can take time outs.

Planned getaways are wonderful and necessary but five or ten minutes of escape to a physical or mental space will work just as well. Use that space to refresh your outlook, boost your energy and focus. Life can, and often does, throw us curve balls that knock us off balance, but planned "down time" builds resilience and a healthy attitude during times of stressful change.

Remember, it is not the place; it's your headspace. Only you control that space.

RELIGION AND OR SPIRITUALITY: Practicing your ways to ground and center your life is vital to maintaining or restoring balance and joy. Whatever you believe, make the time to re-enforce its' positive influence on your life. Studying and practicing its' principles allows you to lean on it in times of stress, rejoice with it in happiness or call on it in any situation that you feel you need the guidance of a trusted, reliable source. Your religious or spiritual practice can be a go to source for stability and peace in your life.

It can steady and comfort you as well as reorient you on the path to peace and meaning after a major life challenge. Like anything that is of importance, you must evaluate, nurture, and practice your spirituality and religion for it to have a positive influence on your life. Use your KaMIT Codes Companion Journal to record the frequency and benefit to your self-care.

FAMILY AND FRIENDS: Connecting with family and friends in person is challenging these days. Technology allows us to have instant virtual access to family and friends. However, virtual relationships are no substitute for a warm embrace and an eye-to-eye connection. Because human beings need touch to thrive, planning and goal setting in this foundational area is just as essential as the rest.

When you spend time with family and friends, you make unforgettable memories, and your time together strengthens bonds. Those bonds reinforce your love and appreciation for each other. Virtual connection is another way to spend time with family and friends. If you live far away from family and friends, you can still stay connected with the not so tech-savvy relative via handwritten cards and letters. It takes more effort, but the feelings communicated will be stronger.

Send unexpected small gifts or pick up the phone and call. Do not wait for someone's birthday or special occasion to connect. Make that special effort to connect with those that live far away. Use technology when needed but strive to spend time in person face to face. *Plan* and set goals to increase spending time with family and friends. Write it down and measure your progress.

When all that you have left of them are memories, you can find peace and comfort in the memories and connections made. The bonds of love that you forged will strengthen you to move forward with joy. Plan, schedule, and act. Make time.

WORK AND CAREER Earning an income is essential to provide the basic needs of all living creatures: food, clothing, and shelter. There is nothing wrong with wanting to advance your career or to afford wonderful things. Care and mindfulness of the approach to reach those goals is necessary to prevent work and career from taking priority over living in balance and joy.

When and how to shut down and separate work from your personal life is further complicated with the use of technology in the workplace. All workplace duties are on laptops, accessible anywhere at any time. If explicit rules are not in place and understood by employer and employee, the expectation that you will be available for your job 24/7 without additional compensation can make it harder to prevent job-creep.

During your interview process, ask about after-hours work and compensation. Be clear about what hours you agree to work, and what is the after-hours pay rate? If you are a salaried employee, it is important to set expectations before you accept the position.

Are vacations and retreats off limits from work? Your private life and health can suffer due to the constant added pressures of your job. What can you do to balance the time spent at and on work with other aspects of your life? Set clear boundaries around work. Arrive at your job, perform your assigned tasks, and go home.

Avoid job-*creep*. Job creep is a slow invasion by your career or job into every aspect of your life. To prevent this from happening, be mindful of how often your personal life and your job intersect. Do not take work home or answer calls and emails after hours unless that is a part of your job description. Avoid conversations about your job with family members on a regular basis. It is natural to want to share your workday with a spouse; job creep though, finds you combining your social life and work life in the form of dinners and vacations together with workmates. The lines of separation blur because now you have a social life intricately woven with work life.

If those lines have blurred, set goals, and make plans to clearly separate work from the rest of the foundational elements. Write your plan out in your KaMIT Codes Companion Journal. Set goals to improve based on the assessment you made by looking at one month of data.

For example, if you assessed that you spend on the average two hours online with job related tasks after you leave work, set a goal to gradually reduce that to zero in (x) amount of time. Repeat this with all areas of work until there is a clear, ongoing, measurable work/life balance.

As you begin to make positive changes in your life and see the results, you will still have stress. Change is stressful; it does not matter whether you label it negative or positive.

The known, even though it may not be the best situation, can be preferable to unknown change.

You may be concerned about what others think of you now that you are not as accessible to them. Family and friends, for their own personal reasons, may openly complain about your emerging lifestyle of self-care. You begin to feel guilty for not spending the same amount of time with them as before. Immediately hit the mental pause button, regroup, and remember, you decided to KaMIT; to put yourself first. Say, "I am worth it, and I stand my ground." Repeat until the waves of guilt pass. This will ease your concerns about your choice to take care of yourself first.

An effective and effortless way to counter stress is to practice relaxation techniques. There are a variety of relaxation techniques, and they all reduce tension and much more.

They slow down the heart and breathing rate, which helps to focus the mind. To practice these techniques, you will need 5 to 10 minutes of your time and a quiet space.

Highlighted below are five relaxation techniques that you can practice anywhere at any time. It is important to be aware of the best way to maximize these relaxation techniques. You can adjust suggestions to suit your time and environment.

- **Correct posture**: Sit up straight, feet flat, shoulders relaxed and hands resting on each thigh. If you are sitting on a cushion with your legs in the lotus position, rest your arms at your side and rest your hands on your knees.

- **Sound:** That is your choice. Some find music helpful in focusing their mind. Try both ways and choose what is best for you.

- **Amount of time**: There is no minimum amount of time required. I recommend at least 10 minutes. Increase or decrease the amount of time according to your schedule.

- **Object of your meditation:** You choose what to focus on; an image, object, person, or an event.

# *Mantra:*

*Merriam Webster's definition of mantra: A mantra is a sound, word, or phrase repeated by someone who is praying or meditating. A word or phrase repeated often, that expresses someone's basic beliefs.*

The idea of a mantra is to still the negative self- talk and replace it with words that will center and connect you with a positive intention or aspiring goal. Use your mantra when you want to calm your mind and self-encourage. The words that you choose do not matter if they have a positive meaning for you. Repeat mantras silently or aloud for as long as needed to focus your mind on what you wish to accomplish.

## *Body Awareness:*

Starting from the top of your body, visualize, tense and un-tense the muscles of each body part, breathing slowly and deeply as you do so. Infuse each body part with your favorite color. Repeat for two to three cycles. Another technique that connects you with your body deeply is what I call body appreciation. Focus on each body part beginning with your toes to the top of your head. Say words of appreciation and gratitude for each body part. Express total acceptance for the current state of your body. This is an amazing way to affirm self-love mentally, emotionally, and phys-ically.

## *Counting Backward*

Sit in a chair with your feet flat and your back against the chair, close your eyes. Count down from twenty to one. Inhale and exhale as you visualize each number. Hold for a beat before exhaling. When you get to one, continue to say "one." As you continue to say one, visualize your favorite happy memory or wish. When you open your eyes, continue to visualize that image as if it were right there for you to touch. Let that feeling and image stay with you as you move through your day. This is helpful in imagining what you would like to happen in the future. Imagine how your lifestyle will be when you constantly live in well-being, balance, and joy. While in this state, affirm without limits what you want to have, become, or do.

Spend as much time as you like on KaMIT-Code1. It has taken years of conditioning, repetitions, and re- enforcement to cement your current lifestyle of not prioritizing self-care. It will take effort to dislodge, excavate and clean out old mindsets before you can build a new foundation.

 If you are reading or listening to this information, then the "you" that is rooted in well-being is seeking more ways to practice self-care. Practices like meditation, healthy eating, physical exercise help you keep stress at bay as you grow into your self-care routine. You now can discover and develop the person underneath all the layers of experiences and memories. You gain clarity about current priorities and how they led to you taking a backseat to your own wellbeing is essential.

# The Four KaMIT Codes

It is not necessary to dismiss all the choices from your entire past, which would be impossible, but finding out how they have shaped the person that you are now is essential to you mastering KaMIT Code 1.

Stay consciously aware of all the foundational elements to your well-being, family, work, down time, religion and spirituality, exercise, and nutrition. Be aware of their influence on your well-being. Are they adding or taking away from your well-being? Adjust when necessary.

Consider taking care of yourself as a gift and a privilege, it is not something you need to earn or convince others that you deserve. It is a birthright. A gift that you show appreciation for in the way that you take care of yourself. Be willing to do whatever it takes to consistently practice self-care first. It starts with the right mindset.

Live A Life of Wellbeing, Balance, and Joy!

A mindset is an attitude, a perspective or viewpoint on how you perceive something. Do you believe that you deserve to put yourself first? Ask for help from others if necessary. My sincere hope is that you will KaMIT to taking care of the precious one-of-a-kind creation called you.

Live A Life of Wellbeing, Balance, and Joy!

The 4 KaMIT Codes

*"Harmony: a pleasing combination or arrangement of things."*

*Merriam Webster's Learner's Dictionary.*

What is pleasing to you? What does harmony and balance look like for you?

# KaMIT CODE 2: CREATE HARMONY

It's about how you arrange your headspace more than your physical space.

# The 4 KaMIT Codes

# CODE 2

# Create Harmony

Your lifestyle is representative of your whole being. It informs the outside world about who you are and what you value. Is what you show to the outside world congruent with who you are or aspire to be internally?

How do you begin to know? Of course, there is really no need to impress anyone just for the sake of it, but if your life is in harmony and balanced, you reflect it externally in the way you live your life. KaMIT-Code 2 helps you assess key elements in your environment as to how they influence your lifestyle. The questions to ask yourself throughout your assessment are "are these elements promoting harmony, and are they compatible with the person that I discovered in KaMIT-Code 1"?

Now it is time to incorporate the new self-discovered you that KaMIT Code 1 revealed into your outside daily life. You begin to do that by assessing key elements in your life for harmony. Some common key elements that influence harmony in our life are family, home, friends, job/career, and entertainment.

# Family

Your greatest advocate, family, is comprised of different personalities that sometimes clash with each other. The result is like the sound of an out of tune instrument instead of notes on a melodious scale. Spouses, parents, children, siblings, and extended family members can be loving and supportive individuals in their own unique way. They also can inflict emotional wounds that last a lifetime if we let them.

For example, a family member may live a lifestyle that you would not have chosen. When you see them, you tense up and express your opinions about how they live their life. An argument starts, shouting follows and the meeting ends with both of you angry and even worse, all communication stops. The hurt, sadness, and helplessness that you feel as you repeatedly watch them fall back into injurious behavior makes you want to avoid them all together. Your heart hurts for them.

What is helpful in those situations is to separate the behavior from the person and have a well-defined objective. This will require emotional maturity and clarity of intention. If you were to step back and think about what your real intentions are for offering unsolicited advice, you might find that you wanted to genuinely help.

You might find that you wanted to feel righteous, better than or in control. Did you want to be the rescuer or the person that has all the answers? Whatever your intentions are, it is important to understand why you feel this way and what needs you are trying to fill. Go back to KaMIT-Code 1 and look at where you may be out of balance.

Of course, it is difficult to watch family members make decisions with bad outcomes, but rather than arguing or retreating, try to find common ground. Look for the good. Considering the others' feelings and motives helps defuse volatile situations. If that is not possible, remember KaMIT-Code 1; take care of yourself.

Being clear about your intentions when interacting with family, friends, and loved ones promotes the harmony that you seek. You can only change you, and sometimes the best decision is to limit or eliminate your exposure to family members that constantly disrupt your harmony.

# Home:

One common barrier to having a harmonious living space is clutter, so the removal of clutter is a good place to start. Twice a month assess your living space for harmony and ask yourself if you are pleased. If not, what must change to have a pleasant, organized living space?

Release unwanted or unused items that are taking up space and energy in your home. Donate them to those in need, have a garage sale or take them to the dump if they are beyond use. We all hold on to that outfit for when we lose the extra weight. Have you thought about the stress and worry accumulated about not reaching a future weight goal? It disrupts the harmony you seek.

After you have decluttered your space, stop, and take a minute to check in and process how you feel. Do you feel relief and a sense of lightness after letting go of items that "held you" in the past? How can items hold you? Items can have strong emotional memories tied to them that make you reluctant to part with them. These emotions can evoke negative feelings that you need to release. You start to let go of unwanted memories and emotions when you declutter.

Surround your home with favorite items that create harmony. Use colors, furniture, sounds, plants, pets, and fragrances in ways that feel natural to you. This is not just about your personal decorating style; it is about your well-being while in your home.

How do you know if your home is harmonious; by how it makes you feel when you are in it? Walk into your living space and sense your mood. Use your sense of sight, smell, touch, and hearing to immerse yourself in space. Is there constant noise, and clutter lying around? Are you calm or anxious?

If any unusually strong feelings surface, write them down in your journal. Fully explore them when you have more time. Your home should be a sanctuary for peace and renewal; a place to retreat from the outside environment.

Many of you share your home with family members, so it is vital that you carve out "my space" in your home. Everyone in the home should have such a space. Add favorite things to that space that make you feel happy, safe, and relaxed. Go to that place physically or mentally during stressful times.

A house and a home are two quite different spaces. Houses are structures that segment empty space. Homes are the people, contents and energy that reside there. All structures take on the energy of the people and things that reside inside of them. Ideally, you can feel at home in any structure that has a life-affirming resonance.

You are responsible for doing your part in filling that structure with harmony and keeping it that way. Remember, your mental attitude plays a big part in creating harmony in your home, so take time to declutter your mind as well. Leave the outside confusion outside and be mindful of what type of mental energy you bring into your living space.

# Friends:

We are social creatures. Our social well-being is a vital part of living a life in balance and harmony. We shrink without social interaction. Friends play a significant role in keeping us grounded and emotionally balanced. They function as confidants, psychologists and counselors and we do the same for them. Sometimes, though, friendships become one-sided. We all have a limited supply of time, patience, and energy.

Just the day-to-day living requires our attention, takes up our time, and causes us to experience emotional highs and lows. Friends and family should be a refuge from the daily grind. If you have felt emotionally drained when around certain friends, you may be in a one-sided friendship. Energy draining, unflattering or hurtful comments from friends further tax limited supplies of emotional energy.

Assess if you are in a one-sided friendship. In your KaMIT Codes Companion Journal, make a list of all your friends. Prepare this list with future consequences in mind. This requires an objective, perceptual mindset. This exercise may be challenging to you because of your emotional connection to the people on the list.

List the things that you have in common, and or any disagreements. After the tough times, was trust and respect still there? How was the issue resolved? Are you giving or taking more from the relationship? Put a check mark beside the friend if trust remains. Look at your list and decide if you want someone in your life that you cannot trust, genuinely like, or have outgrown. That is a decision that only you can make. By taking ownership and being accountable for living a harmonious life, you build confidence in your choices.

If you decide to remove a person from your friends list, pull the bandage off quickly. Ouch! There is pain now, but remember your goal is to live a joyful, balanced, harmonious life. If there is a change in your friend's behavior, it is your choice to re-establish a connection or not. They may be on a journey of personal growth as well as you.

# Job and Career:

Companies should have an on-boarding program or orientation for new employees. It is during the interview process that you and the company decide if you are a cultural fit for the company. Being a cultural fit is key to how well you will thrive and advance in your new position. The company and your values should align. If they do not, you may start accepting or tolerating things that disrupt your harmony.

During orientation, you meet key personnel, review policy and procedures, and you get a sense of how you will fit in with the other employees in the company. This is the time to establish clear boundaries. Keep relationships professional. Consciously maintain and respect each other's privacy. Avoid office gossip, office politics, offering unsolicited opinions about co-workers, and taking sides. The company hired you for your skills and talent, so show your appreciation by doing an excellent job.

Be a collaborator, contribute to creating harmony in your work environment when appropriate. Routines, calendars, and task lists are organizational tools that are essential, especially if you work from home. Use them to keep you on task, motivated and goal oriented.

A strong work ethic and a desire to make advances in your job or career are compatible with a harmonious workplace environment. If you conscientiously apply the rules of workplace harmony, they will complement each other.

It is not the environment or the place so much as your mental headspace. Your goal is to be in harmony, as well as create harmony within all your foundational elements. They all contribute to wellbeing, balance, and joy. Workplace harmony is no different or more important than any other.

# Music/Entertainment

Music and entertainment affect and influence everyone's lives in significant ways. Music can inspire, motivate, and uplift, or depress, and incite wrong actions. How it affects you depends on your personal tastes. Each generation has a soundtrack of their life that ties together key moments and emotions in time. Someone from another generation might label that music as rebellious, or strange. Just because they cannot relate or agree with your choice does not invalidate the benefits to your well-being.

The 4 KaMIT Codes are personal for your idea of well-being. There is no need for judgment from others or from yourself about the rightness or wrongness of choices, especially in entertainment. A wonderful aspect of music is its ability to put you in touch with your feelings.

The best way to sense how music affects your mood is to tune in to how your body reacts. Try this out: play one of your favorite songs, especially one from an earlier time in your life. Listening to music from your past can trigger emotions and memories from that moment in time. Reflect on how that music shaped your life and continues to influence you now. Notice how your mood changes. Is it upbeat, optimistic, or inspirational?

What thoughts come to your mind while listening to music? Are they happy, uplifting, or inspiring? Are they dark, sad, or self-defeating? Has your heart rate accelerated or slowed? Is your breathing rate shallow or rapid? What types of images does the music create in your mind? Does the music lift your mood, sooth you and harmonize with your lifestyle or does it make you tense, moody, angry, or irritable?

Write down your feelings, thoughts, and moods in your KaMIT-Code Companion Journal. Choose the ideal music that motivates and energizes you and avoid the rest.

Evaluate all the types of entertainment that you gravitate towards for their positive, harmonious influence in your life. Set goals to eliminate the rest. This is a personal decision that you must make for yourself. If your choice of entertainment does not harm anyone else, always refer to KaMIT-Code 1 which is, "take care of yourself first."

Despite our intention to live a harmonious life, situations arise that create disharmony. Listed below are some workable ideas to correct disharmony.

**Reevaluate** and define the situation by stepping back to a neutral position. The way you define a situation or issue influences how you approach a solution. The great news is that you choose the definition. Reframe the situation by considering everyone's perspectives.

Look for the best solution that does not leave everyone involved feeling like they had to settle for less than harmony. Remember, take care of your well-being.

> "When you change the way, you look at things, the things you look at change." Wayne Dyer.

**Pause:** Take several deep breaths and count to five before you speak, send that text, email, picture, tweet, etc. Pausing allows you time to center and gain clarity.

**Prioritize:** You may have to fulfill various roles; (parent, employee, spouse, business owner), but you cannot effectively fulfill them all at once. Multitasking is sometimes necessary but should be infrequent. Be fully present in what you do. This relates back to the importance of KaMIT-Code 1, "take care of yourself first." Put your "you" hat on first and you will be in a better frame of mind to deal with disharmony when conflicts arise.

**Release:** Give yourself permission to scream and shout in private for five seconds; it is OK. Afterwards, regroup and look for beneficial, harmonious solutions. Always return to and focus on your end goal, harmony in all areas of your life.

It takes time and effort to replace the old automatic reactions with effective new ones. Have patience with yourself and do not lapse into negative self-criticism. Instead say, "I ask for and bless good fortune for myself." You do deserve to live in harmony, so commit to having, living, and enjoying a full life, that's pleasantly arranged and pleasing to you.

It is easy to dismiss or miss when something is not in harmony. We get comfortable in our daily routines. Assess your friends, family, home, and all-important key aspects of your life monthly or more for harmony. Are there any changes that you are hesitating to make at work? Have new friendships emerged that need assessing? Before doing what is necessary to maintain harmony, it is helpful to relax and consciously tune into your body's physical and mental sensations before you do. This puts you in touch with your Voice of Wisdom.

Your V.O.W. or voice of wisdom is your subtle gut instinct that lets your mind know if something is right for you or wrong for you. It is nature's way of alerting us before we take any action. To access your voice of wisdom you must turn off the mental chatter. Use any of the previous relaxation techniques to help aid you in quieting your mind. Use your V.O.W. in all areas of your life. It is a support system that helps you maintain balance, joy, and wellbeing.

*What harmonic note does your life strike?*

*Do you like the tune?*

Live A Life of Wellbeing, Balance, and Joy!

# The 4 KaMIT Codes

Give/ Share

Freely transferring the possession of something to someone.

# KaMIT CODE3:

# GIVE BACK SHARE

Breathe out, breathe in. That's the essence of giving and receiving. Giving and sharing is part of the human blueprint.

# The 4 KaMIT Codes

# CODE 3

# Give Back / Share

Giving and receiving is a constant, dynamic, and vital process which you can find illustrated in all areas of life. For instance, something as basic and vital as breathing in (receiving air) to exhaling (giving back) illustrates this perfectly.

This exchange takes place automatically and unconditionally. When you hold your breath, you interrupt the natural flow of blood, energy, and other life-sustaining processes. If this goes on for too long, death proceeds. Giving back (exhaling) unblocks the two-way life sustaining flow. All giving and receiving is not as vital as the illustration above, but it highlights this principle as something worthy of consideration. That is, when you give and share unconditionally, you always receive something back; sometimes in ways that you do not immediately recognize or think of as beneficial.

You may stop giving because you gave or shared something with others in the past and were disappointed with what you received back or that you did not receive anything back. When that happens, you prevent the natural exchange of positive energy that comes from giving and receiving. It is helpful to remember that the receiving is not always immediate, but you will receive. Frequently it will complement what you gave or shared and in the same spirit in which you gave. Or you may not be able to connect the dots of what your receive back to what you gave. The point is to give out of love, without expectation. What you receive is often not material. For instance, if you share your ability to teach piano to someone without cost, what you receive is joy, happiness, a glad heart, and fond memories. It's those intangible soul expressions that contribute to well-being and balance.

Search your home, local community or around the globe for any opportunities to give and share. Record the results in your Ka-MIT Codes Companion Journal. Put yourself in someone else's shoes and ask yourself what you would want if you were in the same situation. Likely your needs would not be much different from another's. If it is within your discretion and ability to do so, give and share. Giving back and sharing does not mean that you must blow a trumpet ahead of your deeds. Sometimes the recipient may never know what you did for them.

We all have something that we can share, big or small. A small gesture from you could be life changing for someone else. Your kindness may return to you when you least expect it; all you must do is stay open to receiving and be clear about what your intentions are for giving. Accept gratitude from others and consider it as a receiving back.

Below is a valuable list of items that you might not have thought of as giving back and sharing.

# Love

Love, freely given and expressed, has an equal impact on the giver and receiver. It feels right and good to give and receive unconditional love. Think of the love you have for your child, and the lengths you would go to express your love and support. You give your all and you, in return, receive joy and happiness at seeing their success. Give this type of unconditional love to yourself and to others freely. Every day, look for ways to show love.

Express love by not judging, not criticizing, and by keeping opinions about noncritical matters to yourself; especially among family members. Give and show love by treating others the way you want others to treat you. It is as simple, and yet profound, as that.

# Knowledge/Skills

Talent comes in countless forms from countless types of people. Whatever talents you possess, share with others. Most artists will tell you that they freely share their talents because of the joy they themselves receive. Do you know how to play an instrument? Why not play music for someone that you notice is having a tough time? What if you knew someone who wanted to play an instrument but could not afford the lessons? Would you be willing to teach for free or for a small fee?

Are you a good cook, teacher, tailor, speaker, athlete, or a writer? Those are only a few ways to share your talents. Ask yourself, "what talents do I have, and with whom can I uplift with those talents?"

I knew a floral shop owner who would take flowers to nursing homes just to cheer up the workers and the residents. She told me, "I felt more satisfaction from hand delivering those flowers than hopefully the staff and residents did from receiving them."

# Empathy

Showing empathy, compassion and kindness is like handing a fresh glass of ice-cold water to someone lost in the desert. Everyone has had or will have desert (harsh) experiences in their lives. Show empathy towards them and yourself during those times.

Empathy expressed verbally or physically can have a significant impact on others. A kind word spoken at the right time might be just what's needed to encourage someone to endure; to get back up after a fall or to bear the unbearable.

There is a story that I like to repeat about how just a slight nod of the head and a "keep your chin high" gesture from a fitness class instructor encouraged a struggling attendee to ignore rude comments from others.

The small bit of empathy shown, without saying a word, encouraged her to stick with the class and reach a goal that she might not have been able to accomplish had he not shown kindness.

Kindness and compassion, giving and sharing, costs nothing in comparison to the goodwill that they produce. Empathy, compassion, and kindness are priceless, free gifts that everyone can give or share with another.

# Appreciation

Everyone wants to feel appreciated. Show your appreciation by saying thank you often. Say specifically why you are appreciative. Assess whether you take for granted what others do for you. Do you feel you must do things for others because of your role or position? Do you feel others must do certain things for you because of who you are? Do you take for granted the small but important acts that others do on your behalf every day?

Gratitude is another word for appreciation; both mean you have a sense of the value of something. You understand the effort needed to produce the gift that you received.

Show your appreciation by saying thank you often and say specifically why you are appreciative. When you say thank you, it effectively communicates that you know the value of and are appreciative of what someone gave or shared.

You are acknowledging that you see them, not only on the surface for what they gave, but also on a self-affirming level. Heartfelt appreciation will also encourage you to think of valuable ways to share and give back.

# Time

Time is a finite resource so you must decide how and with whom you want to share this gift. The 4 KaMIT Codes encourage balance, so start with how much free time you can share. The pace of your environment may be so fast that you live your life on autopilot. Days, weeks, months and even years go by without registering in your conscience. The 4 KaMIT Codes ask you to be conscious of your day-to-day activities.

Are there unnecessary events and time-consuming, low-payoff tasks on your calendar? Clear the unnecessary ones from your day and consolidate the others. Use the freed-up time to spend with someone or volunteer at an event that needs your time and attention. Are there opportunities to gain experience and expand your awareness in places outside of your usual community?

There is a delicate balance that you must maintain between giving time to outside interest and time spent in introspection.

The spare time that you give, and share volunteering does contribute to your well-being. Time alone in introspection is just as vital to your inner harmony. The space that you created in Ka-MIT- Code 2 is where you can go to decompress, meditate, or pray regularly.

You can balance the two by tuning in to how each impacts your well-being. Balancing these two dynamics requires a conscious awareness of your feelings and moods. Ask yourself, after a difficult day, which do you prefer; quiet introspection or to actively participate in, and lend a hand to an event that will benefit others? After introspection, decide the best way for you to give or share your time in every situation. Your well-being is your top priority.

# Money

Financial abundance is not necessary to give or share your money. Find a charity that you care about and give what you can. The items that you decided to donate when you decluttered your home could raise money during a garage sale. Donate that money to a cause that matters to you. Organizations like Goodwill, The Salvation Army, missions, shelters, and the Red Cross can use material and monetary donations year-round.

Items like blankets during the winter and fans during the summer meet the needs of nonprofit organizations on an ongoing basis. Purchase those items during off season sales and donate them during peak need. Water and other basic supplies are always in demand during times of disasters.

Select your favorite charity and give financially or with other valuable resources like your time and knowledge.

## Advice

If you have expertise or experience in an area that might help someone, do not hesitate to make it known and shared. This saves resources, especially time and money on preventable mistakes. There is nothing like experience, so why waste precious time learning something from the beginning? Often, others just want someone that they can ask for their opinion on certain matters or to discuss ideas. Always ask for permission to share advice and stay within your area of expertise. It is important to stay neutral and non-accusing when giving advice. Lead with a phrase like "if I were you, I would do such and thus." Use us instead of you. Be discreet with privately shared conversations.

The principle of giving and receiving, embedded in us at conception, is a part of the human blueprint. You have the innate ability to live in well-being, balance, and joy. What you give is not as important as the spirit in which you give. It is important that you are clear about why you give. Sharing your talents, knowledge, time, appreciation, advice, and money begrudgingly will not contribute to your joy. Avoid the pressure to give or share just because of outside influence. What, how much, and to whom you give your resources is a personal decision.

The KaMIT Code 3 principle, give back and share, is fundamental to inner joy on a soul level. Joy is a feeling that is difficult to express with words, yet your whole being reflects it in the way you move through life.

The act of giving and receiving create a joyful

cycle that contributes to a life of well-being, balance, and

joy.

The 4 KaMIT Codes

CODE 4

Reaching/ Expanding

"To stretch out, to arrive at or come to something. Synonyms: embracing, encompassing, spanning, spreading to, stretching, touching."

Merriam Webster's Learner's Dictionary.

Live A Life of Wellbeing, Balance, and Joy!

# KaMIT CODE 4: KEEP REACHING

Mental and physical expansion is a natural attribute of being human, yet a considerable number of people experience resistance to change. The KaMIT Code 4 addresses the reasons why resistance to change happens and how to overcome the obstacles that hold you back.

The 4 KaMIT Codes

Live A Life of Wellbeing, Balance, and Joy!

# CODE 4

# Reaching Expansion

Why set new goals for expansion? When you get to a place where you have mastered self-care, created harmony in your life and giving/ sharing are at the level you chose, you may ask yourself "it took me a long time to feel content and in balance, why shake things up?"

Live A Life of Wellbeing, Balance, and Joy!

"Wouldn't it be ok to just be happy and content with where I am?" Have you considered the fact that all life is dynamic and the circumstances and elements surrounding life are always in constant flux, most of them seamless and automatic? Or, you think you have a plan or an intention of how your day will go, but something unexpected happens or someone disrupts your carefully planned day. You must constantly modify and adapt to even the most minor changes. Practicing KaMIT Code 4 teaches you to actively seek change for the sake of expansion, both mentally and physically.

You can practice conscience change by examining an area of your life that is out of harmony. Take a widespread problem that most people have, not enough time for example, and conceive one new way of thinking about and addressing the problem. Should you prepare better, get up earlier or remove items from your to do list?

For every solution you can think of, state a reason one will not work. What comes easier for you to do, produce a solution, or imagine a reason the solution will not work? Years of static thinking and acceptance of the status quo can make it easier to produce reasons why solutions will not work. You might think that you have tried it all and done it all, so why even try something new? The great news is you can reverse that habit with practice. Practice your new solution for twenty-one days and assess your results. Did the solution work? Have you gained more time? Do you look at the situation differently? Are you taking responsibility for the change? If you do not see the desired result, keep modifying and adapting. When you are satisfied with your solutions, look for ways to improve on your previous goals. Set bigger goals.

With today's fast-paced lifestyles, it is easy to miss or willingly ignore that your environment has changed. The environment may have changed in a subtle, small way or a major life-changing way that forces you to respond.

Repeating the same actions using the same tools and methods while expecting different results becomes frustrating. At that point you want and need change, but you hesitate. Why? You willingly ignore the frustration because, like most people, you thrive on stability and routines. Predictability in people, routines, and events are comforting even when they no longer serve your best interests. You may have become so comfortable that you fail to realize that you have stopped growing or have outgrown a relationship, place, or situation.

Fear also plays a significant role in resistance to change. You may fear your inability to meet the challenges that the change requires. One of the simplest, yet hardest, things to do is to say "yes" to change. You might have stepped out on faith before and the results were not what you envisioned. If that is the case, a rallying phrase can motivate you to bounce back.

A rallying phrase is like a mantra; it gives you that moment of clarity that you need to get back up, try again, and continue to reach forward. What word or phrase holds action-inspiring power for you? Is there a favorite quote from someone that you like? If not, create one of your own and use it often. You can go back and review KaMIT-Code 1 for self-encouragement.

Before you can take meaningful action, you must acknowledge that you are stuck. Evaluate your current situation to determine if you are working with an outdated and underperforming mindset. If you conclude that you are not living up to your ideal potential, set goals and make a plan that allows you to enter and thrive in a unique environment.

You might have to acquire new skills and knowledge. You also must expand your comfort zone. Write down your fears. On paper, they may not be as scary or overwhelming as they are in your head. After you have faced your fears, act. When making your plan, think about the skills that you already have or how you can use them.

You do not have to make drastic changes to grow and expand. The innovation of skills that you already possess is another way. Just by tweaking how you approach something or how you think about a situation can have a profound effect on your expansion. Ask yourself, "in what new ways can I use what I already know?" or, "is there something new to learn about a subject or skill that will allow me to reach higher?"

What do you aspire to have, be or do? Do you want to run a marathon, travel all over the world, become a teacher, graduate from college, earn a certain income, or become the president of a country? Once you have your answer and a sound reason, make your plan. In your KaMIT Codes Companion Journal, compare where you are now with where you aspire to be. Record your aspirations, plans, goals, and tactics. You must implement your plan and measure the results.

What steps will you have to take to reach your new goal? How willing are you to try new ways of approaching people, circumstances, and opportunities? Are you willing to think outside of the box to move forward? How will you objectively measure the results? If higher education is the goal, have you enrolled in classes or read books about a particular subject? Has the applied knowledge given you your desired results?

Have the goals that you accomplished allowed you to expand and thrive in your unfamiliar environment? Are these methods repeatable? In other words, how will you know if you have mastered the disciplined ways it took to accomplish them? What is important is that you continue to keep reaching, growing, and moving in ways that bring you balance, well-being and joy.

If you are just beginning any new journey stay open. During the first parts of the journey, assessing, planning, and implementing, you meet mental obstacles because you are retraining your brain. You are also stepping out of your comfort zone. Remember, the brain likes the predictable, so it will resist. Learning curves are natural when you attempt something new. Stay positive if you do not master the change quickly or face obstacles or setbacks.

If you get stuck during any parts of implementing KaMIT Codes 4 use the tactics below to become unstuck.

• Define/assess the current situation. Are you happy with the status quo?

Define (brainstorm) practical solutions.

• What is the outcome that you would like to have? You must have some idea of what the unfamiliar environment will look like.

- Gradually build up your courage; make minor changes first and build on those. You do not have to solve the entire problem at once.

- Listen to your inner V.O.W. (your voice of wisdom).

- Act. Small steps can have a significant impact on your life.

- Stay curious, ask questions, and challenge assumptions. Do not accept the status quo if it no longer brings joy, balance, and well-being into your life.

Aspirations and goals are good for your well-being. They prevent you from resisting the natural flow of change and expansion. Ka-MIT-Code 4 "keep reaching" is a mental and physical principle that keeps your mind agile, and your body prepared for change.

To counteract resistance to change, reframe it. Think of change as experiencing a new adventure. Can you think of change and expansion as an exciting journey full of surprises around every corner? Use phrases like "I get to" experience learning something new instead of "I have to" learn something new. Can you feel the instant mental shift and the feeling of confidence that arises? Of course, you plan for the outcome, but by reframing your approach to change, you bypass the dread that facing change brings.

Mentally practice the "what if" game. Ask yourself "what if I fail in my effort to try something new?" and then always respond with, "what if I do?"

You will have to think of an answer regardless of what question comes next. You get to rehearse scenarios. This mental "what if" game is a tremendous aid towards facing the unknown. Remember, growth and expansion are a natural feature of all living things. You now have The 4-KaMIT Codes as a reliable, practical resource to guide you on your journey. Imagine, unlimited expansion into balance, well-being, and joy. That is what lies ahead for you when you practice and master The 4 KaMIT Codes. Isn't it your time?

Expand, Grow, Reach.

That is the natural movement of all living things.

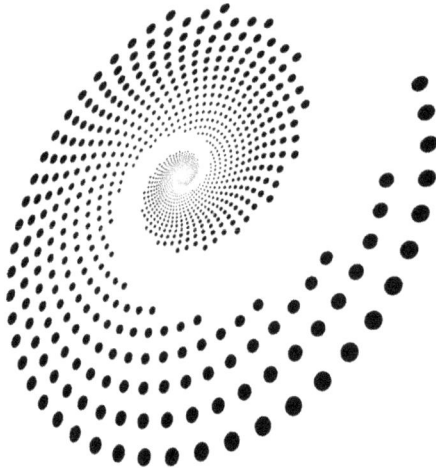

Live A Life of Wellbeing, Balance, and Joy!

The 4 KaMIT Codes

Live A Life of Wellbeing, Balance, and Joy!

# Summary

Living life in balance and well-being is in your hands. It is your birthright. The 4 Codes assist you in realizing this truth. A life of joy, balance and well-being can be yours when you practice the 4 KaMIT Codes; Self-Care, Harmony, Giving and Expansion. These Codes are only words; it is the meaning that you give to those words, the principles that they embody and the actions that you take that will transform your ways of thinking and your life.

If you change your ways of thinking and acting about anything, your life will change. Review and apply the 4 KaMIT Codes often to reinforce your new joyful lifestyle. They will remind and guide you to stay open and in balance with your life's best possibilities.

Always remember, whatever you do, you must commit to it if you want to see results. You must get up, suit up and show up for life. You were born with all that you need to live in balance, well-being, and joy. It is in your DNA. It is y our birthright. May you live the lifestyle that you deserve, One of balance, well-being, and joy.

*One note about having and living a life of well-being, balance, and joy. Sometimes the lifestyle we seek is already present, but we put off living it, always chasing that "intangible perfect thing." Avoid that by consciously embodying the practical life-scaping principles in each of the 4-KaMIT Codes.*

HERE'S TO AN AMAZING LIFE OF WELL-BEING,

BALANCE AND JOY!

Always remember, whatever you do, you must commit to it if you want to see results. You must get up, suit up and show up for life. May you live the lifestyle that you deserve. One of balance, well-being, and joy.

*Dorris Bogus*

www.ingramcontent.com/pod-product-compliance
Lightning Source LLC
Chambersburg PA
CBHW071453070426
42452CB00039B/1260